To Lynn,

Thank you

our second daughter,

Love,

Louise + Vince
Enright

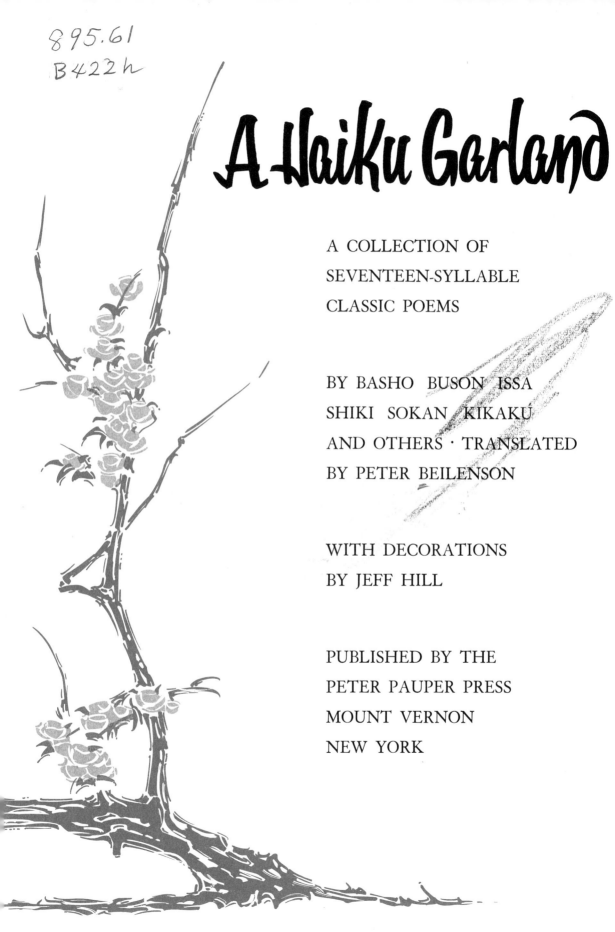

A Haiku Garland

A COLLECTION OF
SEVENTEEN-SYLLABLE
CLASSIC POEMS

BY BASHO BUSON ISSA
SHIKI SOKAN KIKAKU
AND OTHERS · TRANSLATED
BY PETER BEILENSON

WITH DECORATIONS
BY JEFF HILL

PUBLISHED BY THE
PETER PAUPER PRESS
MOUNT VERNON
NEW YORK

A NOTE ON JAPANESE HAIKU

THE *hokku* — or more properly *haiku* — is a tiny verse-form in which Japanese poets have been working for hundreds of years. Originally it was the first part of the *tanka*, a five-line poem, often written by two people as a literary game: one writing three lines, the other, two lines capping them. But the *hokku,* or three-line starting verse, became popular as a separate form. As such it is properly called *haiku,* and is vastly popular among the Japanese.

There are only seventeen syllables in the *haiku,* the first and third lines contain five, the second line seven. There is almost always in it the name of the season, or a key word giving the season by inference. (This is a short-cut, costing the poet only one or two syllables, whereby the reader can immediately comprehend the weather, the foliage, the bird and insect life — and the emotions traditional to the season: factors which almost always are important in the poem.) But there is also, in a good *haiku,* more than a mere statement of feeling or a picture of nature: there is an implied identity between two seemingly different things.

The greatest of *haiku*-writers, and the poet who crystallized the style, was Basho (1644-1694). In his later years he was a student of Zen Buddhism, and his later poems, which are his best, express the rapturous awareness in that mystical philosophy of the identity of life in all its forms. With this awareness, Basho immersed himself in even the tiniest things, and with religious fervor and sure craftsmanship converted them into poetry. He was ardently loved by his followers, and by later poets, and his Zen philosophy has thus been perpetuated in later *haiku.*

Following Basho in time and fame was Buson (1715-1783) — a little more sophisticated and detached than his predecessor, and an equally exquisite craftsman. The third great *haiku* poet was unhappy Issa (1763-1827), a continual butt of fate. He is less poetic but more lovable than Basho and Buson. His tender, witty *haiku* about his dead children, his bitter poverty, his little insect friends, endear him to all. Other masters are of course represented here too.

It is usually impossible to translate a *haiku* literally and have it remain a poem, or remain in the proper seventeen-syllable form. There are several reasons for this. *Haiku* are full of quotations and allusions which are recognized by literate Japanese but not by us; and are full of interior double-meanings almost like James Joyce. And the language is used without connecting-words or tenses or pronouns or indications of singular or plural — almost a telegraphic form. Obviously a translation cannot be at once so illusive and so terse.

In the *texture* of the poems there is a further difficulty: Japanese is highly polysyllabic. The only way to reproduce such a texture in English is to use Latinized words — normally less sympathetic than the Anglo-Saxon. For all these reasons, the following versions make no pretense to be literal or complete, and some variations in the five-seven-five syllable arrangement have been allowed.

Alterations and interior rhymes, which are common in Japanese because every syllable ends with one of the five vowel sounds (sometimes with the addition of the letter "n") have been freely used; but as in the originals, there are no end-rhymes except some accidental ones.

One final word: the *haiku* is not expected to be always a complete or even a clear statement. The reader is supposed to add to the words his own associations and thus to become a co-creator of his own pleasure in the poem. It is hoped that our readers may here co-create such pleasure for themselves!

PETER BEILENSON

A Haiku Garland

Spring

Such a fine first dream...
But they laughed at me...they said
I had made it up

Takuchi

Even my plain wife...
Exquisite as visitors
On New Year's morning

Iso

New Year-gift-giving...
Ah, baby at her bare breast
Reaching tiny hands

Issa

First wind of the year...
The oil-lamp in the washroom
Shudders and is still

Oemaru

Felicitations!
Still...I guess this year too
Will prove only so-so

Issa

Year's first cart-load...
Cut-out paper flowers deck
The emaciated horse

Shiki

First dream of the year...
I kept it a dark secret...
Smiling to myself

Sho-u

Sun-melted snow...
With my stick I guide this great
Dangerous river

Issa

From my tiny roof
Smooth...soft...still-white snow
Melts in melody

Issa

Icicles and water
Old differences dissolved...
Drip down together

Teishitsu

Old snow is melting...
Now the huts unfreezing too
Free all the children

Issa

A childless housewife...
How tenderly she touches
Little dolls for sale

Ransetsu

Now wild geese return...
What draws them crying crying
All the long dark night?

Roka

Pouring floods of rain...
Won't Mount Fuji wash away
To a muddy lake?

Buson

Clear-colored stones
Are vibrating in the brook-bed...
Or the water is

Soseki

In my new clothing
I feel so different I must
Look like someone else

Basho

Oh you bawdy breeze…
Thatcher bending on the roof
I see the bottom!

Issa

Immobile Fuji…
Alone unblanketed by
Millions of new leaves

Buson

Spring morning marvel…
Lovely nameless little hill
On a sea of mist

Basho

Passing the doll shop
I picked up the littlest one . . .
Suddenly I smiled

Baishitsu

There in the water
Color of the water moves . . .
Translucent fishes

Raizan

Hazy ponded moon
And pale night sky are broken . . .
Bungling black frog

Buson

Silver-soft riverside . . .
Dim splash of far-thrown net . . .
Fishing for the moon?

Taigi

Paper-weights protect
Gay picture-books in the shop...
Inquisitive breeze
                    Kito

Ah-ah-ah-choo! that
Spring catarrh!...now I've lost sight
Of my first skylark
                    Yayu

An April shower...
See that thirsty mouse lapping
River Sumida
                    Issa

Rainfall in April...
Tears from our weeping willow...
Petals from our plum
                    Shoha

Ah little warbler
Thanks-droppings on my porch
Because I love you?

Basho

Under my tree-roof
Slanting lines of April rain
Separate to drops

Basho

Farmer, raise your head...
Direct this stranger who will smile
And disappear

Buson

Good morning, sparrow...
Writing on my clean veranda
With your dewy feet

Shiki

Beach fishermen go
Bobbing out . . . beach poppies stay
Bending with sea-breeze

Kyorai

Even the ocean
Rising and falling all day . . .
Sighing green like trees

Buson

I could not see him
That fluttering fly-off bird . . .
But the plum-petals . . .

Shiki

Gliding river boat . . .
Rising skylarks . . . rippling sounds
To our right and left

Ranko

Bird-droppings pattern
The purples and the yellows of
My iris petals
                    Buson

Shining on the sea...
Dazzling sunlight shaking over
Hills of cherry-bloom
                    Buson

Over the low hedge
Honest plum distributes petals
Half inside...half out
                    Chora

Riverbank plum-tree...
Do your reflected blossoms
Really flow away?
                    Buson

Blue evening sea...
From Spring islands near and far
New lights are shining
                    Shiki

The old messenger
Proffering his plum-branch first...
Only then the letter
                    Kikaku

Midnight full of stars...
Dim cherry-petals floating on
Rice-paddy waters
                    Buson

Over my shoulder...
My friends who followed me were lost
In clouds of blossom
                    Chora

The seashore temple...
Incoming rollers flow in time
To the holy flute
                    Buson

Low-tide morning...
The willow's skirts are trailed
In stinking mud
                    Basho

Here comes Mr. Horse...
Quick, quick, out of the roadway
Happy sparrowlet
                    Issa

Moonlight stillness
Lights the petals falling...falling...
On the silenced lute
                    Shiki

Green...green...green...
Willow-leaf threads are sliding
River-running-water

Onitsura

Cherry-petal days...
Birds with two legs glitter now
Horses gleam with four

Onitsura

Heat-wavelets rising...
Plum-petals drifting wavering
Down on burning rocks

Shiki

Come now, play with me...
Fatherless motherless dear
Little sparrow-child

Issa

No bold rain-cloud for
A hundred miles around...dares
Brave the peonies

Buson

In the clear fording
Pale feet of the silent girl...
Clouding May waters

Buson

Opening thin arms...
A pink peony big as this!
Said my bitty girl

Issa

Ultra-pink peony...
Silver Siamese soft cat...
Gold-dust butterfly...

Buson

Energetic ant...
Silhouetted on the still
Snowflake peony

Buson

In the yard plum-trees
Blossom...in the brothel
Girls are buying obis

Buson

That white peony...
Lover of the moon trembling
Now at twilight

Gyodai

Facing the candle
The peony also burning...
Motionless at death

Kyoroku

The first firefly...
But he got away and I...
Air in my fingers

Issa

Listen, all you fleas...
You can come on pilgrimage, O K...
But then, off you git!

Issa

But if I held it...
Could I touch the lightness of this
Flutter-butterfly?

Buson

Hanging sadly down
Amid the merry-makers...
Green weeping willow

Roka Shonin

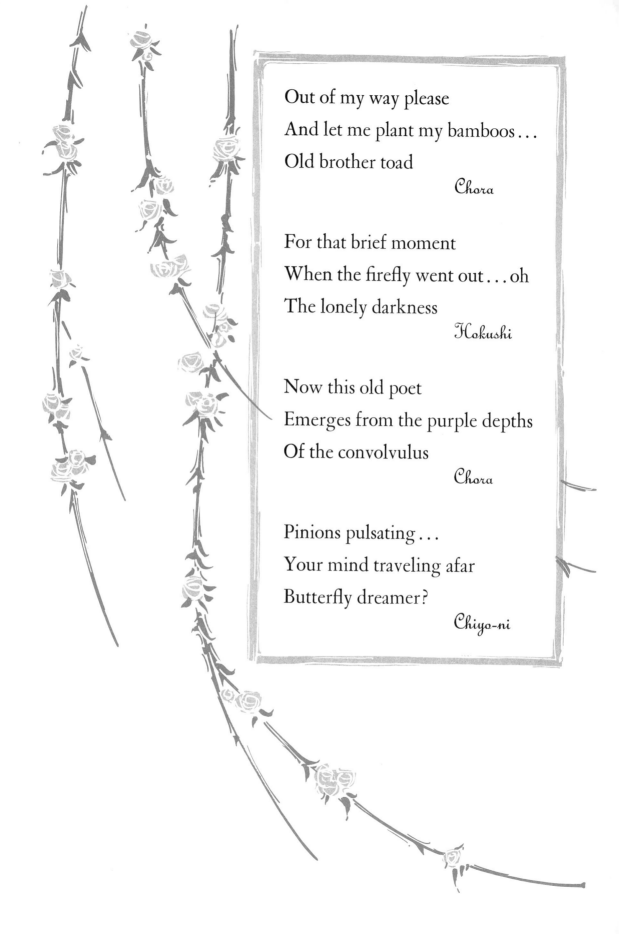

Out of my way please
And let me plant my bamboos...
Old brother toad

Chora

For that brief moment
When the firefly went out...oh
The lonely darkness

Hokushi

Now this old poet
Emerges from the purple depths
Of the convolvulus

Chora

Pinions pulsating...
Your mind traveling afar
Butterfly dreamer?

Chiyo-ni

Moon-in-the-water...
Broken-again...broken-again...
Still a solid seal

Choshu

Now having taken
Warmed water...the vase welcomes
My camellia

Onitsura

Fallen now to earth
After dancing journeyings...
Kite that lost its soul

Kubonta

Keeping company
With us, pigeons and sparrows...
Low-tide-lookers all

Issa

What, traveling
In the rain?...but where can he
Be wending snailward?

Issa

NEW YEAR'S EVE

I can snore in peace...
The New Year won't confront me
Till tomorrow noon

Buson

New Year's Day...poet
Though I be I'll proudly wear
My father's scabbard

Kyorai

In the New Year dawn
Solemn and deliberate
Tall cranes go marching

Kikaku

From the mountain pass
See the sunlit castle town . . .
Flying New Year kites
                        Taigi

Seeing my birth-cord
Kept at our old native place . . .
New Year's Day I wept
                        Basho

No you don't! get out! . . .
Thus they warmly welcomed me
To their New Year feast
                        Rotsu

Snow is melting . . .
Far in the misted mountains
A caw-cawing crow
                        Gyodai

Spring at early dawn...
On the tips of barley leaves
Little last pale frost

Onitsura

Up from April snow
Rising udo sprouts...tender
Purple succulent

Basho

At dear Basho's grave
Pale thin transients we pause...
Spring mist, sad pupil

Joso

Hear those baby mice
Huddled in their nest...peeping
To the sparrowlets

Basho

Above the hamlet:
Green the silent bamboo-grove...
White lingering snow
                    Taigi

Spring cobalt ocean...
Across snow-white mountains fly
Black returning birds
                    Shiki

Immediately...
On their Spring return tireless
Swallows zig-zagging
                    Taigi

See: our candlelight
Illuminates the sapling's
Fresh-unfolded gold
                    Buson

Troops of tourists come
For April flower-viewing...
Oh, they're sparrow-men

Basho

Gusty Spring breezes...
But the stubborn plum buds still
Gripping their thin twigs

Onitsura

Spring unfolds anew...
Now in my second childhood
Folly, folly, too

Issa

Bony brushwood twigs
Cut down and stacked in bunches...
Yet bravely budding

Boncho

Placing the kitten
To weigh her on the balance . . .
She went on playing

Issa

Spring evening beach . . .
Helping fishermen unload
Living sea-treasure

Ranko

It is Spring again . . .
Gay in the garden gather
Sun-bathing sparrows

Onitsura

Tremendous forces . . .
Stone-piled fence all tumbled down
By two cats in love

Shiki

After the shower...
Spring-enchanted sparrow-folk
Chatter on the eaves

Uko

Silent cherry-bloom...
Again with your old eloquence
Address my inner ear

Onitsura

Having scoured my skin
And bowed my skull to Buddha...
Now for cherry-bloom!

Issa

Afternoon garden...
Planting perhaps seven seeds...
I'm convalescent!

Shiki

This baby...even
When we show him cherry buds...
Opens eager lips

Seifu-jo

Mountain-top of clouds
Towering behind the hedge...
Or a flowering plum?

Shiro

Dancing: the fox treads
Among the pale narcissi
In garden moonlight

Buson

After Spring sunset
Mist rises from the river...
Spreading like a flood

Chora

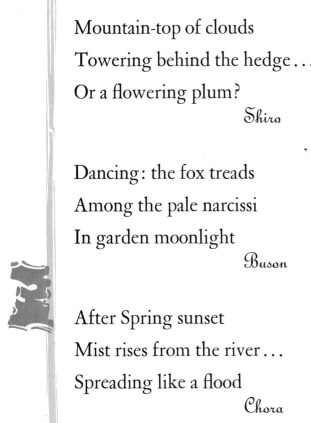

Then the peonies
Extinguishing all others...
Opened their petals

Ki-Ichi

Endless Maytime rain...
Sneaking back one night, the moon
Perched in the pine-tree

Ranko

Now that I am old
Even tender days of Spring
See...can make me cry

Issa

Beautiful lady
Buffeted by rude Spring winds...what
Sweet storm you make!

Kito

On the shining roof
The boy's abandoned string-ball
Soaking up Spring rain

Buson

Sweet Spring shower...
Enough to wet the tiny shells
On this little beach

Buson

Ere Spring guests arrive
We light the supper candles
Each from shining each

Buson

Dull-dreary rain-day...
Dripping past my gate a girl
Bearing irises

Shintoku

Yes: the young sparrows
If you treat them tenderly...
Thank you with droppings
Issa

Following the bank...
For miles no river-spanning bridge
This long Spring day
Shiki

At Takiguchi
Voices calling for a light...
Darkening Spring rain
Buson

Pattering shower...
They are putting out the lamps
All down doll-shop lane
Buson

Flooded paddy-fields...
The lake has come to town all green
With seedling rice

Bakusui

Vanishing Springtime...
Wistfully the lonely widow
Pouts at her mirror

Seibi

Blown cherry-blossoms
Fall and float upon the cold
Rice-paddy waters

Kyoroku

The gay waterwheel
In the valley pours petals
From mountain cherries

Chogetsu

In these dark waters
Drawn up from my frozen well . . .
Glittering of Spring

Ringai

Standing still at dusk
Listen . . . in far distances
The song of froglings!

Buson

I dreamed of battles
And was slain . . . oh savage Samurai!
Insatiable fleas!

Kikaku

In silent mid-night
Our old scarecrow topples down . . .
Weird hollow echo

Boncho

Women planting rice...
Ugly every bit about them...
But their ancient song
                    Raizan

Wild geese write a line
Flap-flapping across the sky...
Comical Dutch script
                    Soin

Dead my old fine hopes
And dry my dreaming but still...
Iris, blue each Spring
                    Shushiki

In this windy nest
Open your hungry mouth in vain...
Issa, stepchild bird
                    Issa

Ballet in the air...
Twin butterflies until, twice white
They meet, they mate
                    Basho

ON THE DEATH OF HIS CHILD
Dew evaporates
And all our world is dew...so dear,
So fresh, so fleeting
                    Issa

Black cloudbank broken
Scatters in the night...now see
Moon-lighted mountains!
                    Basho

Seek on high bare trails
Sky-reflecting violets...
Mountain-top jewels
                    Basho

For a lovely bowl
Let us arrange these flowers...
Since there is no rice

Basho

Now that eyes of hawks
In dusky night are darkened...
Chirping of the quails

Basho

My two plum trees are
So gracious...see, they flower
One now, one later

Buson

One fallen flower
Returning to the branch?...oh no!
A white butterfly

Moritake

Cloudbank curling low?
Ah! the mountain Yoshino . . .
Cherry cumulus!

Ryota

Fie! this fickle world!
Three days, neglected cherry-branch
And you are bare

Ryota

Hanging the lantern
On that full white blooming bough
Exquisite your care!

Shiki

April's air stirs in
Willow-leaves . . . a butterfly
Floats and balances

Basho

In the sea-surf edge
Mingling with bright small shells...
Bush-clover petals

Basho

THE RIVER

Gathering May rains
From cold streamlets for the sea...
Murmuring Mogami

Basho

A gate made all of twigs
With woven grass for hinges...
For a lock...this snail

Issa

Wind-blown, rained on...
Bent barley-grass you make me
Narrow path indeed

Joso

Arise from sleep, old cat,
And with great yawns and stretchings
Amble out for love
                    Issa

White cloud of mist
Above white cherry-blossoms...
Dawn-shining mountains
                    Basho

Hi! my little hut
Is newly-thatched I see...
Blue morning-glories
                    Issa

In the city fields
Contemplating cherry-trees...
Strangers are like friends
                    Issa

See, see, see! oh see!
Oh what to say? Ah Yoshino...
Mountain-all-abloom!
                    Teishitsu

Green shadow-dances...
See our young banana-tree
Pattering the screen
                    Shiki

Don't touch my plumtree!
Said my friend and saying so...
Broke the branch for me
                    Taigi

Twilight whippoorwill...
Whistle on, sweet deepener
Of dark loneliness
                    Basho

Reciting scriptures…
Strange the wondrous blue I find
In morning-glories
                    Kyoroku

Many solemn nights
Blond moon, we stand and marvel…
Sleeping our noons away
                    Teitoku

Mountain-rose petals
Falling, falling, falling now…
Waterfall music
                    Basho

Amorous cat, alas
You too must yowl with your love…
Or even worse, without!
                    Yaha

The laden wagon runs
Bumbling and creaking up the road
Three peonies tremble

Buson

Ah me! I am one
Who spends his little breakfast
Morning-glory gazing

Basho

My good father raged
When I snapped the peony...
Precious memory!

Tairo

By that fallen house
The pear-tree stands full-blooming
An ancient battle-site

Shiki

In the open shop
Paperweights on picture books...
Young Springtime breeze

Kito

Dim the grey cow comes
Mooing mooing and mooing
Out of the morning mist

Issa

Take the round flat moon
Snap this twig for handle...
What a pretty fan!

Sokan

Seas are wild tonight...
Stretching over Sado Island
Silent clouds of stars

Basho

Why so scrawny, cat?
Starving for fat fish or mice...
Or backyard love?

Basho

Dewdrop, let me cleanse
In your brief sweet waters...
These dark hands of life

Basho

Lightning flash, crash...
Waiting in the bamboo grove
See three dew-drops fall

Buson

Ashes my burnt hut...
But wonderful the cherry
Blooming on my hill

Hokushi

Life? Butterfly
On a swaying grass that's all...
But exquisite!

Soin

Glorious the moon...
Therefore our thanks dark clouds
Come to rest our necks

Basho

What a peony...
Demanding to be measured
By my little fan!

Issa

Under cherry-trees
Soup, the salad, fish and all...
Seasoned with petals

Basho

Now from cherry-trees...
Millions of maidens flying
Fierce war-lord storm

Sadaiye

Moon so bright for love!
Come closer, quilt...enfold
My passionate cold!

Sampu

Too curious flower
Watching us pass, met death...
Our hungry donkey

Basho

Clouds of cherry-bloom...
Tolling twilight bell...temple
Ueno? Asakura?

Basho

Must Springtime fade?
Then cry all birds...and fishes'
Cold pale eyes pour tears

Basho

Oh that Summer moon!
It made me go wandering
Round the pond all night

Basho

Chanting and humming
Gongs immerse the green valley
In cool waves of air

Kyorai

My dear pilgrim hat,
You must accompany me
To view the plum trees!

Basho

On this well-worn stone
Garlanded with pinks of Spring . . .
Oh to drink and doze!

Basho

He who climbs this hill
Of flowers finds here a shrine
To the kind goddess

Basho

If I could bundle
Fuji's breezes back to town . . .
What a souvenir!

Basho

Cherry blossoms, yes
They're beautiful . . . but tonight
Don't miss the moon!

So-in

The oak tree stands
Noble on the hill even in
Cherry blossom time

Basho

Poppy petals fall
Softly quietly calmly
When they are ready

Etsujin

When a nightingale
Sang out, the sparrow flew off
To a further tree

Torin

Under a Spring mist,
Ice and water forgetting
Their old difference...

Teitoku

Who cares to notice
Carrot flowers, when plum trees
Explode into bloom!
Sodo

Among these lovely
Cherry blooms, a woodpecker
Hunts for a dead tree
Joso

Even in castles
I have felt the searching breath
Of the wintry wind
Kyoroku

New Year dawning clear . . .
Cheerful sparrows chatter
All day like people
Ransetsu

I'm very sorry
To have to die at this time
With plum trees in bloom
                    Raizan

Even the general
Took off his armor to gaze
At our peonies
                    Kikaku

A year has gone by
And still I've not yet learned
My new master's name
                    Raizan

Summer

With my new clothing
Alas...Spring has been buried
In that wooden chest
                Saikaku

Hands upon the ground
Old aristocratic frog
Recites his poem
                Sokan

As I picked it up
To cage it...the firefly
Lit my finger-tips
                Taigi

Fleeing the hunter
The firefly took cover...
The evening moon
                    Ryota

Softly folded fawn
Shivers, shaking off the butterfly...
And sleeps again
                    Issa

The heavy wagon
Shook all the roadside...waking
A single butterfly
                    Shoha

In the golden room
Frightened quick calligraphy...
Escaping swallow
                    Buson

He wades the river
Carrying the girl and see...
Carrying the moon

Shiki

For deliciousness
Try fording this rivulet...
Sandals in one hand

Buson

Elegant singer
Would you further favor us
With a dance...oh frog?

Issa

Before the sacred
Mountain shrine of Kamiji...
My head bent itself

Issa

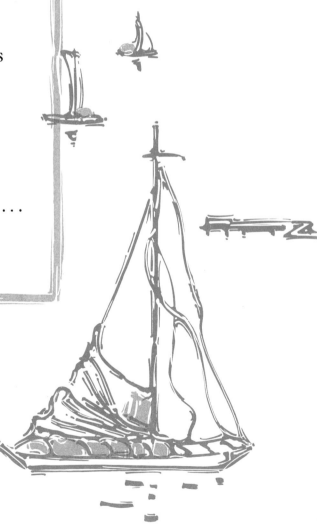

Rainy afternoon . . .
Little daughter you will never
Teach that cat to dance
                        Issa

On the low-tide beach
Everything we stoop to pick . . .
Moves in our fingers
                        Chiyo-ni

Flower-petal fell . . .
Then the rooster crowed, and see . . .
Another petal
                        Baishitsu

Dark the well at dawn . . .
Rising with the first bucket . . .
Camellia-blossom
                        Kakei

Now take this flea:
He simply cannot jump . . . and
I love him for it

Issa

The floating heron
Pecks at it till it shatters . . .
Full-moon-on-water

Zuiryu

For a companion
On my walking trip . . . perhaps
A little butterfly

Shiki

Ah good Buddhist frog . . .
Rising to a clearer light
By non-attachment

Joso

Bats come out at dusk . . .
Woman over the way . . . why
Do you stare at me?

Buson

Overhanging pine . . .
Adding its mite of needles
To the waterfall

Basho

Squads of frogs jumped in
When they heard the plunk-plash
Of a single frog

Wakyu

Little silver fish
Pointing upstream moving down
In clear quick water

Soseki

Look...the palace...
You can glimpse it through that hole
In the mosquito-fog
                    Issa

Congratulations
Issa!...you have survived to feed
This year's mosquitoes
                    Issa

In your Summer-room...
Garden and mountain going too
As we slowly walk
                    Basho

Just beyond the smoke
Of our smudge this evening...
Mosquito-music
                    Shirao

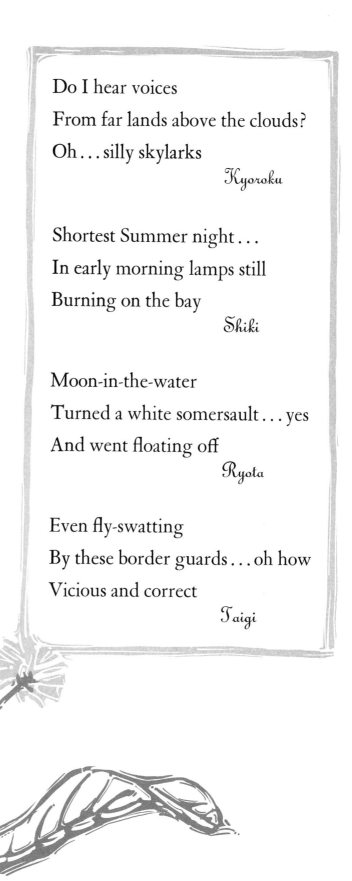

Do I hear voices
From far lands above the clouds?
Oh...silly skylarks

Kyoroku

Shortest Summer night...
In early morning lamps still
Burning on the bay

Shiki

Moon-in-the-water
Turned a white somersault...yes
And went floating off

Ryota

Even fly-swatting
By these border guards...oh how
Vicious and correct

Taigi

Quick-pattering rain...
Chance and vanity dictate
Gay impromptu hats

Otsuyu

You hear that fat frog
In the seat of honor, singing
Bass? ... that's the boss

Issa

Windy-web spider
What is your silent speaking ...
Your unsung song?

Basho

And each morning
Right above this little roof ...
My private skylark

Joso

Don't waste precious time
Now, tagging along with me . . .
Brother butterfly

Issa

Experimenting . . .
I hung the moon on various
Branches of the pine

Hokushi

Swat softly softly
At the sick-room flies . . . because
I seek for sleep

Shiki

The devoted clerk . . .
Not to waste a jot of breeze
Naps on a ledger pillow

Issa

On his garden path
This sparrow scatters pebbles . . .
Man forgotten
                    Shoha

River Mogami
Winding from northern mountains
Washes warm Summer
                    Shiki

Summer-night insects
Falling burnt and dead . . . upon
My poem's paper
                    Shiki

You are just too late
To help with the lamp . . . my moth
Light-extinguisher
                    Issa

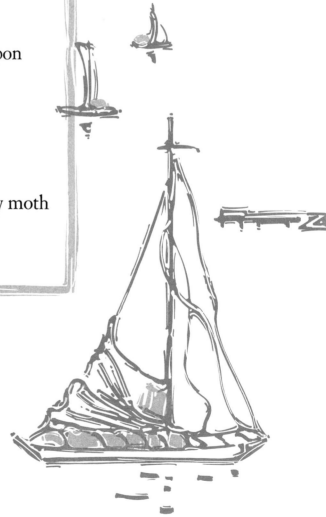

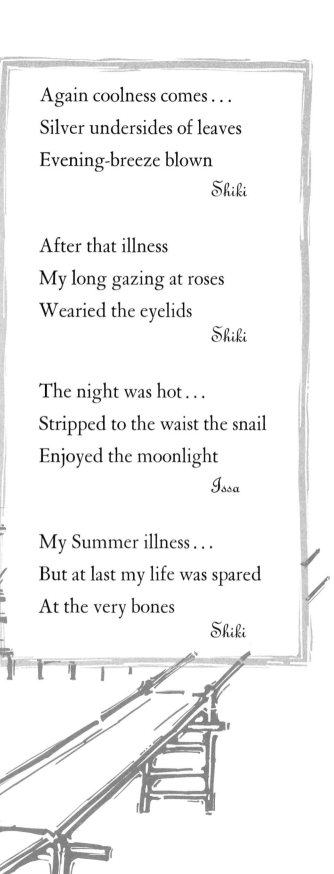

Again coolness comes . . .
Silver undersides of leaves
Evening-breeze blown

Shiki

After that illness
My long gazing at roses
Wearied the eyelids

Shiki

The night was hot . . .
Stripped to the waist the snail
Enjoyed the moonlight

Issa

My Summer illness . . .
But at last my life was spared
At the very bones

Shiki

Careful, champion flea
And look before you leap...
Here's River Sumida

Issa

Coming from the bath...
Cool on her breasts the warm breeze
Of the veranda

Shiki

Fui! a sour plum...
Thin eyebrows pinched together
On the lovely face

Buson

Holy noon duet:
Basso-snoring priest...devout
Contralto-cuckoo

Shiki

Farther in the grove
The lantern walks ... nearer nearer
Sings the nightingale

Shiki

With the new clothes
Remember ... the crow stays black
And the heron white

Chora

I scooped up the moon
In my water bucket ... and
Spilled it on the grass

Ryuho

Must you come to vex
My sick eyes that still can move ...
Bed-criss-crossing fly?

Shiki

Coolness on the bridge...
Moon, you and I alone
Unresigned to sleep

Kikusha-ni

In the endless rain
Is it turning sunward still...
Trusting hollyhock?

Basho

Hot slow afternoon...
Suddenly the hand has stopped...
Slow-falling fan

Taigi

In Summer moonlight
They go visiting the graves...
Savoring the cool

Issa

In the morning breezes
Climbing in a single line
Go singing skylarks

Ryota

A near nightingale...
But my head just couldn't fit
Through the lattices

Yaha

A Summer shower...
Along all the street, servants
Slapping shut shutters

Shiki

Rainfall and thunder
Beating on boards and blossoms...
Indiscriminate

Sampo

Rain-obliterated...
The river, some roofs,
A bridge without a shore

    Basho

O Springtime twilight...
Precious moment worth to me
A thousand pieces

    Sotoba

REPLY:

O Summer twilight...
Bug-depreciated to a
Mere five hundred

    Kikaku

Bouncing bamboo dipper
In the water-tub following
A fly-away bird

    Horo

Ah roadside scarecrow
We've hardly started gabbing...
And I have to go

Izen

A baby sparrow...
Hopping with curiosity
To watch my brushwork

Shoha

How cool...sweet grasses
Scythed in fields at early dawn
Entering our gate

Boncho

On the giddy swing...
Tiny girl-child clutching tight
Her spray of blossoms

Issa

Perhaps this voiceless
Wanderer dreams of flowers...
Butterfly dozer

Reikan

Sometimes the farmer
Trots out to see his scarecrow...
Slowly he walks back

Buson

That dark waterfowl
Although appearing weighted...
See how it can float!

Onitsura

Ah bold nightingale...
Even before his lordship
You won't mend your song

Issa

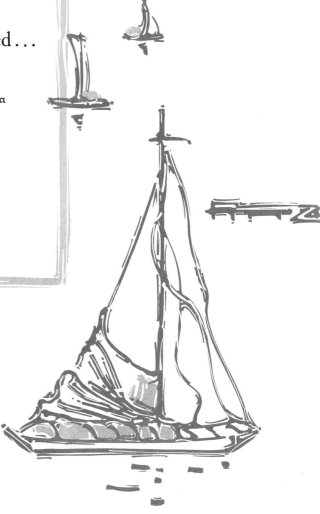

That fat old bull-frog
Sat there staring back at me
With a sour face
Issa

In flat sunset light
A butterfly wandering
Down the city street
Kikaku

Someone is walking
Over the wooden bridge ... hear
The deep frog-silence
Ryoto

A wagon rumbling ...
And out from silent grasses
A sudden butterfly
Shoha

Into the blinding
Setting sun the scarecrow stares...
Still indifferent

Shirao

Gay...affectionate...
When I'm reborn I pray to be a
White-wing butterfly

Issa

Squatting like Buddha:
But bitten by mosquitoes
In my nirvana

Oemaru

At the ancient shrine
Tarnished gold-foil; and green leaves
Awakening time

Chora

Even with insects ...
Some are hatched out musical ...
Some, alas, tone-deaf

Issa

Planted rows of beans
And random clumps of lilies ...
Prosperous islet!

Shiki

Nightingale weeping
And ceaseless ocean moaning ...
Soon oh soon the dawn

Shirao

In Summer moonlight ...
Glittering brooklet running
Down our village street

Shirao

Two jade-green hilltops
Stand in their Summer leafage
Mirror-images
                    Kyorai

Yellow firefly...
Little lamp-flame that to the
Human touch is chill
                    Shiki

Sunny fields and warm...
See the monk's face peeping out
From the temple fence
                    Issa

A crablet crawling
Up my ankle-bone...ah cool
Meandering brook
                    Basho

In my native place
There's this plant: as plain as grass
But blooms like heaven

Issa

Pitiful blind child...
And so brief the Rose of Sharon
Garlanding her porch

Shirao

Daylight at the inn...
Through my looped mosquito nets
A morning-glory

Shiro

Twilight watering...
And please, a cooling sprinkle
For wrens and crickets

Kikaku

Having tumbled off
His grass-blade . . . the firefly
Buzzes up again

Basho

Moonlight nightingale
Casts a whistling line of sound
Over the millpond

Basho

As lightning flashes . . .
Zig-zag screeches of the heron
Flying in the dark

Basho

Hereby I assign,
In perpetuity, to wit:
To this bird this fence

Issa

Stubborn woodpecker...
Still hammering at twilight
At that single spot
                    Issa

At silent noontide...
Far across the flower-fields
Hear the sighing sea
                    Buson

Hear the humming
As honeysuckle petals fall...
Disturbed mosquitoes
                    Buson

The sickly orchid
That I tended so...at last
Thanks me with a bud
                    Taigi

Pot-imprisoned now...
Palely dreaming octopus
In Summer moonlight
                Basho

Curled on the fan...
Aha! I've caught you tom-cat
Fast asleep again!
                Issa

High sun still burning
In the falcon's eyes...down to
My earth-bound wrist
                Taira

But see the mountain...
Shaking with the waves of heat
Where day has gone
                Onitsura

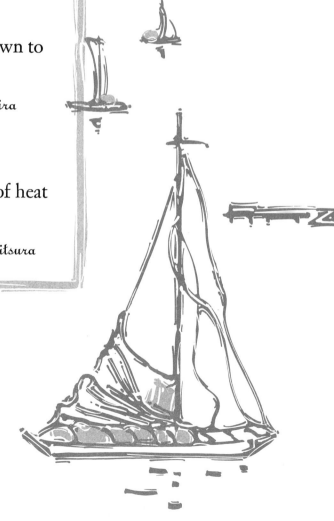

What a monster kite!
Even the bravest eagle
Would not dare attack!

Shiki

Yellow butterfly . . .
Fluttering fluttering on
Over the ocean

Shiki

Cool on blue water
That overhanging islet
With its pine askew

Shiki

What a cooling breeze!
Now all stifled grasshoppers
Gaily sing again

Issa

I will not forget
This lonely savor of my life's
One little dewdrop
                    Basho

Moonlight slanting
Through all this long bamboo grave
And nightingale song
                    Basho

In the rain-pinked pond
Still-unslaughtered silly ducks
Rejoice with quacking
                    Issa

Sparrow family...
Playing at hide and seek
In the tea-bushes
                    Issa

Twilight flower-field...
Moonrise in the eastern sky
Sunset in the west

Buson

Night is darkening...
Silent in the paddy pool
Shines the Milky Way

Izen

On that inch of land

Beans grew to our very door...

Yet grand in moonlight!

Issa

With me on the cliff

Another poet...fellow-guest

Of the Summer moon

Kyorai

Inquiring wren
Looking here and looking there...
Have you lost your bag?

Issa

The sadness of it...
Under the hero's helmet,
Tarnished now, a cricket

Basho

Two water-lilies
Shining serenly golden...
Raindrop-dimpled pool

Buson

While the bobolink
Sings cheerily he gives my shack
The cold critic's eye

Issa

Floating butterfly
When you dance before my eyes...
Issa, man of mud

Issa

Supernatural
Cool breeze...Buddha's paradise
Must lie thataway

Issa

Insects poor insects...
How wise to purge your karma
Crying penitence

Otokuni

We hark to cricket
And to human chirpings...with
Ears so different

Wafu

Slow hot silent hours...
In the afternoon a pheasant
Settles on the bridge
                    Buson

The soft Summer moon...
Who is it moves in white there...
On the other bank?
                    Chora

At my hut I fear
All I can really tempt you with...
Smallish mosquitoes
                    Basho

While I swoop my net
Deliberate butterfly
You never hurry
                    Garaku

Ah...morning-glory
Glowing with the indigo
Of some mountain pool

Buson

Silent the garden
Where the camellia-tree
Opens its whiteness

Onitsura

From the day it's born
Of abandoned sticks and rags...
Elderly scarecrow

Nyofu

Now this good sea-slug
Has both head and tail...but God
Knows which is which

Kyorai

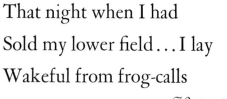

That night when I had
Sold my lower field...I lay
Wakeful from frog-calls

Hokushi

Hey! why don't you help
That buzzing horse-fly open
The sticking skylight?

Issa

Dawn-twittering birds...
Our overnight big-city guest
Alone is stirring

Shoha

Tender bamboo-shoots
And baby's tender gum-pinks...
Tiny tooth-cutting

Ransetsu

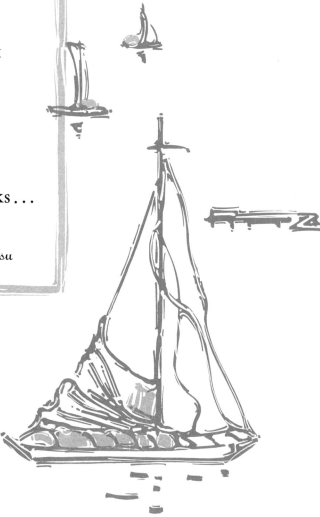

Bouncing the ball...
She bends to make a face at her
Meowing kitten

Issa

In the sudden burst
Of Summer rain, wind-blown birds
Clutching at grasses

Buson

Like a butterfly...
The pilgrim's tomboy youngster
Trots unevenly

Shiki

The monks exhibit
Buddha's image...sparrows too
Are dawn-light lookers

Issa

A nursemaid scarecrow...
Frightening the wind and sun
From playing baby

Issa

ON HER DEAD SON
In what windy land
Wanders now my little dear
Dragonfly hunter?

Chiyo-ni

A saddening world:
Flowers whose sweet blooms must fall
As we too, alas...

Issa

Describe plum-blossoms?
Better than my verses...white
Wordless butterflies

Reikan

Lend me water please?
Some fresh young morning-glory,
Careless . . . took my well

Chiyo-ni

A YOUNG SISTER

Pitiful . . . on my
Outstretched palm at dusk dies
The little firefly

Kyorai

You stupid scarecrow!
Under your very stick-feet
Birds are stealing beans!

Yayu

Afternoon shower . . .
Walking and talking in the street:
Umbrella and raincoat!

Buson

In the farther field
A scarecrow kept me company . . .
Walking as I walked

Sanin

Pretty butterflies . . .
Be careful of pine-needle points
In this gusty wind!

Shusen

Ah, unrequited love!
Now elevate your chin and keen
Tom-cat, to the moon!

Kyorai

Hi! kids mimicking
Cormorants . . . you are more like
Real cormorants than they!

Issa

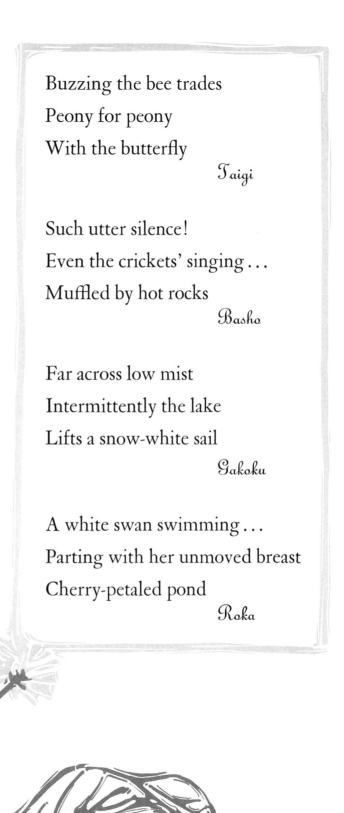

Buzzing the bee trades
Peony for peony
With the butterfly

Taigi

Such utter silence!
Even the crickets' singing ...
Muffled by hot rocks

Basho

Far across low mist
Intermittently the lake
Lifts a snow-white sail

Gakoku

A white swan swimming ...
Parting with her unmoved breast
Cherry-petaled pond

Roka

For a cool evening
I hired the old temple porch . . .
Penny in the dish
                    Shiki

Quite a hundred gourds
Sprouting from the fertile soul . . .
Of a single vine
                    Chiyo-ni

Swallow in the dusk . . .
Spare my little buzzing friends
Among the flowers
                    Basho

Old dark sleepy pool . . .
Quick unexpected frog
Goes plop! watersplash!
                    Basho

My shadowy path
I've swept all day and now…oh no!
Camellia-shower!

Yaha

Hard the beggar's bed…
But sociable and busy
With insect-talking

Chiyo-ni

Come come! come out!
From bogs old frogs salute the dark
And look…the stars!

Kikaku

Over the mountain
Bright the full white moon now smiles
On the flower-thief

Issa

Starting to call you:
Come watch these butterflies . . .
Oh! I'm all alone
                    Taigi

Good friend grasshopper
Will you play the caretaker
For my little grave?
                    Issa

A lost child crying
Stumbling over the dark fields . . .
Catching fireflies
                    Ryusui

The snake departed
But the little eyes that glared . . .
Dew, shining in the grass
                    Kyoshi

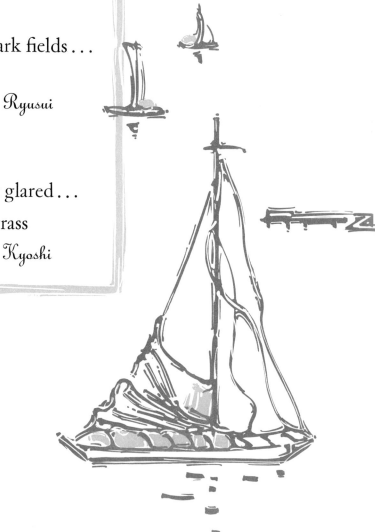

Ah! brave dragon-fly...
Taking for your perch this swatter
Consecrate to death
Kohyo

I raised my knife to it:
Then walked empty-handed on...
Proud Rose of Sharon
Sampu

Giddy grasshopper
Take care...do not leap and crush
These pearls of dewdrop
Issa

Darting dragon-fly...
Pull off its shiny wings and look...
Bright red pepper-pod
Kikaku

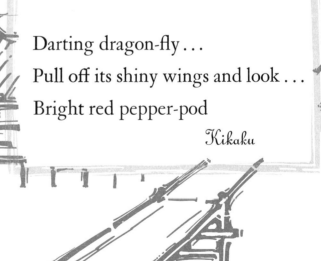

REPLY:

Bright red pepper-pod...
It needs but shiny wings and look...
Darting dragon-fly!

        Basho

Tiny sentences
Brushing soft on my shutters...
Bush-clover voices

        Sesshi

Mirror-pond of stars...
Suddenly a Summer shower
Dimples the water

        Sora

Sadness at twilight...
Villain! I have let my hand
Cut that peony

        Buson

In dim dusk and scent
A whiteness now half hidden ...
Evenfall orchid

Buson

Now be a good boy
Take good care of our house ...
Cricket my child

Issa

Wake! the sky is light!
Let us to the road again ...
Companion butterfly!

Basho

Stillness ... then the bat
Flying among the willows
Black against green sky

Kikaku

Now my loneliness
Following the fireworks...
Look! a falling star!
Shiki

Stupid hot melons...
Rolling like fat idiots
Out from leafy shade!
Kyora

For morning-glories
I can foresee grave danger...
Single-stick practice
Chora

Can't it get away
From the sticky pine-branches...
Cicada singing?
Gijoens

Silent the old town...
The scent of flowers floating...
And evening bell

Basho

Vendor of bright fans
Carrying his pack of breeze...
Suffocating heat!

Shiki

Voices of two bells
That speak from twilight temples...
Ah! cool dialogue

Buson

Deep in dark forest
A woodcutter's dull axe talking...
And a woodcutter

Buson

Camellia-petal
Fell in silent dawn... spilling
A water-jewel
                    Basho

In the twilight rain
These brilliant-hued hibiscus...
A lovely sunset
                    Basho

Friend, that open mouth
Reveals your whole interior...
Silly hollow frog!
                    Anon.

Butterfly asleep
Folded soft on temple bell...
Then bronze gong rang!
                    Buson

Good evening, breeze!
Crooked and meandering
Your homeward journey

Issa

See the morning breeze
Ruffling his so silky hair . . .
Cool caterpillar

Buson

Oh lucky beggar! . . .
Bright heaven and cool earth
Your Summer outfit

Kikaku

The turnip farmer rose
And with a fresh-pulled turnip . . .
Pointed to my road

Issa

FLOWER IN THE STREAM

Thus too my lovely life

Must end, another flower

To fall and float away

Onitsura

I am going out…

Be good and play together

My cricket children

Issa

Not a voice or stir…

Darkness lies on fields and streets

Sad: the moon has set

Imozeni

Lady butterfly

Perfumes her wings by floating

Over the orchid

Basho

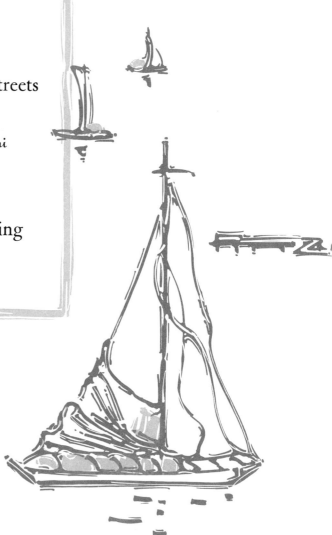

If strangers threaten
Turn into fat green bullfrogs...
Pond-cooling melons

Issa

Yellow evening sun...
Long shadow of the scarecrow
Reaches to the road

Shoha

A camellia
Dropped down into still waters
Of a deep dark well

Buson

For the emperor
Himself he will not lift his hat...
A stiff-backed scarecrow

Dansui

In the holy dusk
Nightingales begin their psalm . . .
Good! the dinner-gong!

Buson

Live in simple faith . . .
Just as this trusting cherry
Flowers, fades, and falls

Issa

Night is bright with stars
. . . Silly woman, whimpering:
Shall I light the lamp?

Etsujin

Black desolate moor . . .
I bow before the Buddha
Lighted in thunder

Kakei

Dirty bath-water
Where can I pour you?...insects
Singing in the grass

Onitsura

Wee bitter cricket
Crying all this sunny day...
Or is he laughing?

Oemaru

A short Summer night...
But in this solemn darkness
One peony bloomed

Buson

Long the Summer day...
Patterns on the ocean sand...
Our idle footprints

Shiki

Angry I strode home . . .
But stooping in my garden
Calm old willow-tree
                    Ryota

Oh do not swat them . . .
Unhappy flies forever
Wringing their thin hands
                    Issa

See . . . the heavy leaf
On the silent windless day . . .
Falls of its own will
                    Boncho

Rash tom-cat lover . . .
Careless even of that rice
Stuck to your whiskers
                    Taigi

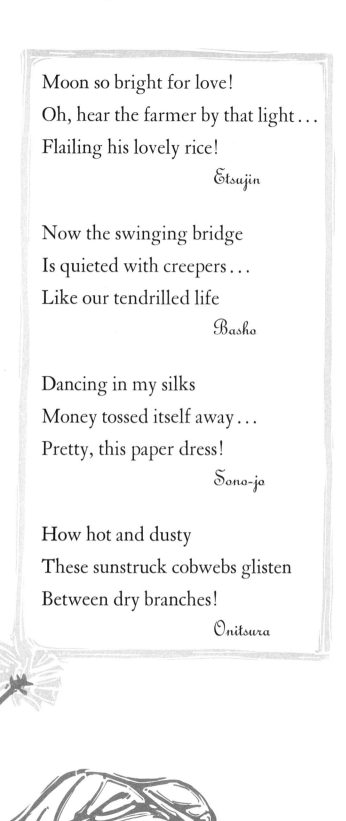

Moon so bright for love!
Oh, hear the farmer by that light...
Flailing his lovely rice!

Etsujin

Now the swinging bridge
Is quieted with creepers...
Like our tendrilled life

Basho

Dancing in my silks
Money tossed itself away...
Pretty, this paper dress!

Sono-jo

How hot and dusty
These sunstruck cobwebs glisten
Between dry branches!

Onitsura

Unknowingly he
Guided us over pathless hills
With wisps of hay
                    Basho

My eyes following
Until the bird was lost at sea
Found a small island
                    Basho

Do the tea-pickers
Also hidden among leaves
Hear the cuckoo's song?
                    Basho

In my small village
Even the flies aren't afraid
To bite a big man
                    Issa

Oh the tiny cry
Of a pitiful cricket
Caught in a hawk's beak!

Ransetsu

Cuckoo, did you cry
To frighten away my mother
Watching in my dream?

Kikaku

Poor crying cricket
Perhaps your little husband
Was caught by our cat

Kikaku

Everything I touch
With tenderness, alas
Pricks like a bramble

Issa

Autumn

In lantern-light
My yellow chrysanthemums
Lost all their color
Buson

Morning-misted street...
With white ink an artist brushes
A dream of people
Buson

At Nara Temple...
Fresh-scented chrysanthemums
And ancient images
Basho

An old tree was felled...
Echoing, dark echoing
Thunder in the hills

Meisetsu

THE GREAT FIRE OF KANDA

Heat-waves to heaven...
Rising from the ruined hearts of
Three thousand homes

Shiki

Chanting at the altar
Of the inner sanctuary...
A cricket priest

Issa

Sad twilight cricket...
Yes, I have wasted once again
Those daylight hours

Rikei

A sudden shower...
Terrified, loud idiot ducks
High-tailing home
                    Kikaku

My melons that you
Stole last year...this year I place
Upon your grave, my son
                    Oemaru

On these rainy days
That old poet Ryokan
Wallows in self-pity
                    Ryokan

Pitiful...fearful...
These poor scarecrows look like men
In Autumn moonlight
                    Shiki

We stand still to hear
Tinkle of far temple bell...
Willow-leaves falling
　　　　　　Basho

The evening breezes...
Water lapping lightly on
The heron's leg-sticks
　　　　　　Buson

The wet kingfisher
Shakes his feathers in the late
Reflected sunlight
　　　　　　Tori

In unending rain
The house-pent boy is fretting
With his brand-new kite
　　　　　　Shoha

The calling bell
Travels the curling mist-ways . . .
Autumn morning
Basho

Nightlong in the cold
That monkey sits conjecturing
How to catch the moon
Shiki

Dark unending night . . .
Once, outside the paper screen,
A lantern passing
Shiki

They have gone . . . but
They lit the garden lantern
Of their little house
Shiki

On one riverbank
Sunbeams slanting down . . . but on
The other . . . raindrops

Buson

Supper in Autumn . . .
Flat light through an open door
From a setting sun

Chora

September sunshine . . .
The hovering dragonfly's
Shimmering shadow

Karo

Do I dare depend
Upon you for firm friendship
Dear morning-glory?

Basho

A windblown grass...
Hovering mid-air in vain
An Autumn dragonfly

Basho

Now the old scarecrow
Looks just like other people...
Drenching Autumn rain

Seibi

Here is the dark tree
Denuded now of leafage...
But a million stars

Shiki

Up from my illness
I went to the chrysanthemums...
How cold they smelled!

Otsuji

Waking in the night
I added my Autumn coughing
To insect voices

Joso

Jagged candle-flame...
The very shape of Autumn sifts
Through the shutters

Raizan

Urging on my horse
Into mist-blanketed water...
River-gurgle sounds

Taigi

White chrysanthemums
Making all else about them
Reflected riches

Chora

Peacefulness...today
Fujiama stands above us
Mist-invisible

Basho

Smack-ack...smack-ack...
Men driving fish-net stakes
In white-fog morning

Buson

White Autumn moon...
Black-branch shadow-patterns
Printed on the mats

Kikaku

Exquisite the dewy
Bramble...to every thorn
A single droplet

Buson

From the temple steps
I lift to the Autumn moon
My veritable face

Basho

In this solid mist
What are those people shouting
Between boat and hill?

Kito

Nights are getting cold . . .
Not a single insect now
Attacks the candle

Shiki

His hat blown off . . .
How pitiless the pelting
Storm on the scarecrow

Hagi-jo

In my own village
I think there are more scarecrows left
Than other people
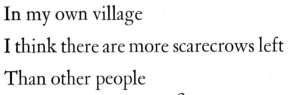
                    Chasei

Swallows flying south ...
My house too of sticks and paper
Only a stopping-place
                    Kyorai

After moon-viewing
My companionable shadow
Walked along with me
                    Sodo

After the windstorm
Foraging for firewood ..
Three fierce old women
                    Buson

Roadside barley-stalks
Torn by our clutching fingers...
As we smiled farewell

Basho

Suddenly chill Fall . . .
Why should the ragged fortune-teller
Look so surprised?

Buson

All the world is cold...
My fishing line is trembling
In the Autumn wind

Buson

Autumn breezes shake
The scarlet flowers my poor child
Could not wait to pick

Issa

Seeking in my hut
For unlocked midnight treasures.
A cricket burglar
                    Issa

On the ebb-tide beach
The hurrying crab stops short...
There is a footprint!
                    Rofu

Braced in the waters...
Scarecrow in the flooded field
Grimly endures it
                    Shiki

Ah my forest hut...
Where the friendly woodpecker
Knocks at door and post
                    Basho

On this still water
See where his reflection
Meets the waterfowl
                    Mahara

Quite the stupidest
Of all living creatures is
A dry old scarecrow
                    Shiki

Autumn nights are cold...
Crushing the tiny child to me...
Warm lovely youngling
                    Shiki

Behind the twisted
Branches with the eagle's nest...
Red sinking sun-ball
                    Boncho

As I light the lamp
Behold...to every single doll
Its own real shadow
                        Shiki

Mother lost, long gone...
At the deep dark sea I stare...
At the deep dark sea
                        Issa

Ah sacred swallow...
Twittering out from your nest in
Great Buddha's nostril
                        Issa

Tea-kettle handle...
I'll cut it from the bamboo
Of that bubbling wren
                        Kikaku

Weeping . . . willows
Kneel here by the waterside
Mingling long green hair
            Kyorai

Gathering starlings
Cry as they sprinkle berries
From the Autumn tree
            Shiki

Silvery herrings
Pouring . . . a live waterfall
From net to basket
            Kikaku

Ah leafless willow . . .
Bending over the dry pool
Of stranded boulders
            Buson

Oh you snub-nose doll!
Maybe your mother didn't
Pinch and pull enough
                    Buson

Perched on the bamboo
Marker of a new-dug grave...
The waiting dragonfly
                    Kito

All along the beach ...
Plovers playing at some game
Involving wet-foot
                    Buson

With philosophy
He contemplates the mountain ...
Old professor frog
                    Issa

At the setting sun...
Washing down his weary horse
In the Autumn sea
                    Shiki

On this plain of mist
Nothing but flat endlessness...
And red-rising sun
                    Shiro

Rising harvest moon...
From this hut as yet unwalled
I will view it well
                    Shirao

Bitter broken reeds...
Day in day out the fallen
Float away...afar
                    Ranko

Penetrating hot
September sun ... on my skin
Feel the cooling breeze

Basho

I am growing old ...
Oh sweet bird disappearing
Into Autumn dusk

Basho

Who is that, huddled
In a straw-coat ... staring at our
Holiday parade?

Basho

See this dragonfly ...
His face is practically
Nothing else but eyes

Chisoku

Companion cuckoo...
Keep your eye cocked on my hut
Until I come back

Issa

Reddish morning sky...
Rain for you today I guess,
Little lucky snail!

Issa

Within pale silence
Spreading from evening moonlight
Sudden cicada

Hajin

Wet morning garden...
My sunny chrysanthemums
Are sea-mist-shrouded

Sampu

With the moon-rising...
Leaf after leaf after leaf
Falls fluttering down
Shiki

I didn't enter...
But I stopped in reverence...
Autumn-leaf temple
Buson

Sudden radiance...
After October rainstorm
Re-reddened peppers
Buson

The people, we know...
But these days even scarecrows
Do not stand upright
Issa

Only withered grasses
In your cage?...oh cricket captive
My apologies!

Shoha

From fish-boat torches
Sparks are falling...poor tethered
Scorch-face cormorants

Kakei

This is my own place...
Mud-hut and companion tree
Shedding Autumn leaves

Chora

From the haunted hut
Smoke is seeping in the rain...
Someone is inside!

Buson

September lightning...
White calligraphy on high
Silhouettes the hill
                    Joso

See...six gaping beaks
Waiting for the mother-bird
In cold Autumn rain
                    Issa

Silent Autumn air...
Here and there among the hills
Rising thin blue smokes
                    Gyodai

The fisherman's hut...
Where lively crickets mingle now
With drying shrimp
                    Basho

ANNIVERSARY OF DEATH

Rising Autumn moon...
Lighting in my lap this year
No pale sickly child

Onitsura

For fall festivals
Our religious dragonflies
Don red garments too

Issa

Wild geese oh wild geese
Were you little fellows too... when
You flew from home?

Issa

By abandoned roads
This lonely poet marches
Into Autumn dusk

Basho

The sea darkening...
Oh voices of the wild ducks
Crying, whirling, white
Basho

White moth, flutter off:
Fly back into my breast now
Quickly, my own soul!
Wafu

Nine times arising
To see the moon whose solemn pace
Marks only midnight yet
Basho

Watching, I wonder
What poet could put down his quill
A pluperfect moon!
Onitsura

Do your worst, old frost
You can no longer wound me...
Last chrysanthemum!

Oemaru

Pebbles shining clear,
And clear six silent fishes...
Deep Autumn water

Buson

A bright Autumn moon...
In the shadow of each grass
An insect chirping

Buson

You turn and suddenly
There in purpling Autumn sky...
White Fujiami!

Onitsura

Here, where a thousand
Captains were victorious...tall
Grass their monument
                    Basho

Yellow Autumn moon...
Unimpressed the scarecrow stands
Simply looking bored
                    Issa

White chrysanthemum...
Before that perfect flower
Scissors hesitate
                    Buson

Cruel Autumn wind
Cutting to the very bones...
Of my poor scarecrow
                    Issa

Now in late Autumn
Look, on my old rubbish-heap...
Blue morning-glory
Taigi

A single cricket
Chirps, chirps, chirps, and is still; my
Candle sinks and dies
Anon.

Fireworks ended
And spectators gone away...
Ah, how vast and dark!
Shiki

Two ancient pine-trees...
A pair of gnarled and sturdy hands
With ten green fingers
Ryoto

I must turn over ...
Beware of local earthquakes
Bedfellow cricket!
Issa

Oh! I ate them all
And oh! what a stomach-ache ...
Green stolen apples
Shiki

Now in sad Autumn
As I take my darkening path ...
A solitary bird
Basho

At our last parting
Bending between boat and shore ...
That weeping willow
Shiki

At Furue in rain
Gray water and gray sand...
Picture without lines

Buson

Oh sorry tom-cat
Bigger blacker knights of love
Have knocked you out!

Shiko

The old fisherman
Unalterably intent...
Cold evening rain

Buson

While I turned my head
That traveler I'd just passed...
Melted into mist

Shiki

Visiting the graves...
Trotting on to show the way...
Old family dog
                    Issa

Will we meet again
Here at your flowering grave...
Two white butterflies?
                    Basho

So enviable...
Maple-leaves most glorious
Contemplating death
                    Shiko

Shocking...the red of
Lacquered fingernails against
A white chrysanthemum
                    Chiyo-ni

Dry cheerful cricket
Chirping, keeps the Autumn gay...
Contemptuous of frost

Basho

Deepen, drop, and die
Many-hued chrysanthemums...
One black earth for all

Ryusui

Before boiled chestnuts
Cross-legged lad is squatting...
Carved wooden Buddha

Issa

Defeated in the fray
By bigger battlers for love...
Tom-cat seeks a mouse

Shiko

Asking their road...
Seven yellow bamboo hats
All turned together
                    Anon.

Torches! Come and see
The burglar I have captured...
Oh! my eldest son!
                    Sokan

Autumn mosquitoes
Buzz me, bite me...see, I am
Long prepared for death
                    Shiki

Nice: wild persimmons...
And notice how the mother
Eats the bitter parts
                    Issa

Gray marsh, black cloud . . .
Flapping away in Autumn rain
Last old slow heron
                    Anon.

First white snow of fall
Just enough to bend the leaves
Of faded daffodils
                    Basho

What a gorgeous one
That fat sleek huge old chestnut
I could not get at . . .
                    Issa

None broke the silence . . .
Nor visitor nor host . . . nor
White chrysanthemum
                    Ryota

If you were silent
Flight of herons on dark sky . . .
Oh! Autumn snowflakes!

Sokan

Chilling Autumn rain . . .
The moon, too bright for showers,
Slips from their fingers

Tokuku

Rainy-month, dripping
On and on as I lie abed . . .
Ah, old man's memories!

Buson

November sunrise . . .
Uncertain, the cold storks stand . . .
Bare sticks in water

Kakei

From dark windy hills
Voices driving weary horses...
Shouting of the storm

Kyokusui

Slanting lines of rain...
On the dusty samisen
A mouse is trotting

Buson

Oh former renter
I know it all, all...down to
The very cold you felt

Issa

Gray moor, unmarred
By any path...a single branch...
A bird...November

Anon.

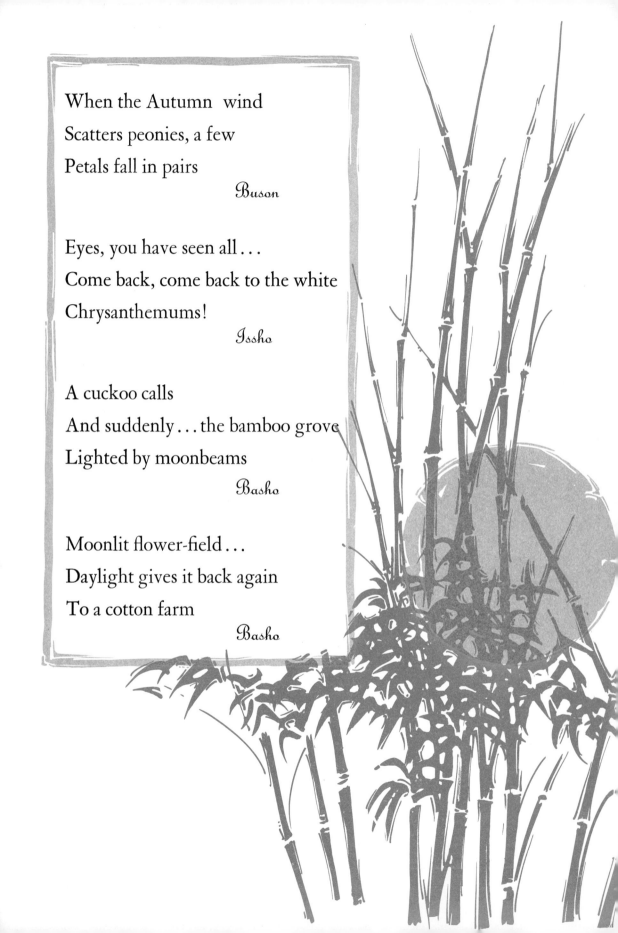

When the Autumn wind
Scatters peonies, a few
Petals fall in pairs
                    Buson

Eyes, you have seen all . . .
Come back, come back to the white
Chrysanthemums!
                    Issho

A cuckoo calls
And suddenly . . . the bamboo grove
Lighted by moonbeams
                    Basho

Moonlit flower-field . . .
Daylight gives it back again
To a cotton farm
                    Basho

Having spoken ill
My lips now feel the cold of
Autumn's fatal wind
                    Basho

Some poor villages
Lack fresh fish or flowers . . .
All can share this moon
                    Saikaku

Unchanged by Autumn's
Icy winds . . . the chestnut's shell
Stays gleaming green
                    Basho

No wonder today
All the men need mid-day naps . . .
Oh that Autumn moon!
                    Teitoku

This old hat, stolen
From a scare-crow...how fiercely
The cold rain pelts it!

Kyoshi

If my grumbling wife
Were still alive I just might
Enjoy tonight's moon

Issa

Unmoved, the melons
Don't seem to recall one drop
Of last night's downpour

Sodo

Now the dragonflies
Cease their mad gyrations...
A thin crescent moon

Kikaku

Pine tree silhouette
Painted by the harvest moon
On a shining sky

Ransetsu

Well, the fall typhoon
Has taken its first victim...
The local scarecrow

Kyoroku

A leaf is falling...
Alas alas another and another
Falls

Ransetsu

Winter

Little orphan girl…
Eating a lonely dinner
In Winter twilight
                    Shohaku

In the wintry moon
Gales raging down the river
Hone the rock-edges
                    Chora

The new-laid garden…
Rocks settling in harmony
In soft Winter rain
                    Shado

When I raised my head...
There was my rigid body
Lying bitter cold
                    Seibi

Over wintry fields
Bold sparrow companies fly
Scarecrow to scarecrow
                    Sazanami

Bath-tub firewood...
Thanks for this final service
Faithful old scarecrow
                    Joso

My very bone-ends
Made contact with the icy quilts
Of deep December
                    Buson

Poor thin crescent
Shivering and twisted high...
In the bitter dark
                    Issa

So lonely...lovely...
The exquisite pure-white fan
Of the girl I lost
                    Buson

In Winter moonlight
A clear look at my old hut...
Dilapidated
                    Issa

Black calligraphy
Of geese...pale printed foothills...
For a seal, full moon
                    Buson

In my dark Winter
Lying ill ... at last I ask
How fares my neighbor?

Basho

The old dog lies intent
Listening ... does he overhear
The burrowing moles?

Issa

A thousand roof-tops
A thousand market-voices ...
Winter-morning mist

Buson

First snow last night ...
There across the morning bay
Sudden mountain-white

Shiki

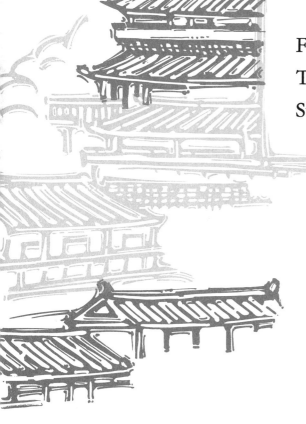

When the waterpot
Burst that silent night with cold...
My eyes split open

Basho

Winter having touched
These fields...the very tomtits
Perch on the scarecrow

Kikaku

Cold Winter rainfall...
Mingling all their gleaming horns
Oxen at the fence

Ranko

See the red berries...
Fallen like little footprints
On the garden snow

Shiki

Winter-evening snow...
The uncompleted bridge is all
An arch of whiteness
                    Basho

Moonlit snowfields...
Here the bloodied samurai
Cast their noble lives
                    Kikaku

Midnight Wanderer
Walking through the snowy street
Echoing dog-bark
                    Shiki

As to icicles
I often wonder why they grow
Some long...some short
                    Onitsura

In Winter moonlight
Fish-net stakes cast their shifting
Uneven shadows
                    Shirao

Colder far than snow...
Winter moonlight echoing on
My whitened hair
                    Joso

So close...so vast...
Rattling Winter hailstones on
My umbrella-hat
                    Basho

Long-walking lantern
Disappeared into some house...
Desolate white hills
                    Shiki

Solitary crow...
Companioning my progress
Over snowy fields

Senna

Staring delighted
Even at walking horses
In new morning snow

Basho

Blinding wild snow
Blows, whirls and drifts about me...
In this world alone

Chora

Winter moonlight casts
Cold tree-shadows long and still...
My warm one moving

Shiki

In that cold darkness
My horse stumbled suddenly
Just outside the house
                    Buson

Look at that stray cat
Sleeping . . . snug under the eaves
In the whistling snow
                    Taigi

In my New Year heart
I feel no fury . . . even at
These tramplers of snow
                    Yayu

Coffin and mourners
Passed me walking down the street
Midnight at New Year's
                    Shiki

To celebrate New Year's
We feast newly-opened eyes on
Snowy Fujiama

Sokan

DEATH-SONG:

Poet nightingale...
Will I hear your later verses
In the vale of death?

Anon.

DEATH-SONG:

Suddenly you light
And as suddenly go dark...
Fellow-firefly

Chine-jo

DEATH-SONG:

Full-moon and flowers
Solacing my forty-nine
Foolish years of song

Issa

DEATH-SONG:

If they ask for me
Say: he had some business
In another world

          Sokan

Tell me: where does this
Unexpected cold snap come from . . .
Weather-wise scarecrow?

          Issa

Wine-drinking-wakeful
All alone that bitter night
I stared at snowfall

          Basho

Snow-isolated . . .
Once more I press my back against
My thinking-post

          Basho

Back to my home town
And burial in my hut...
Five cold feet of snow
                    Issa

Winter woodcutter...
When your axe cuts home I scent
Unexpected Spring
                    Buson

My old father too
Gazed out on these white mountains
Through lonely winters
                    Issa

Feeble feeble sun...
It can scarcely stretch across
Winter-wasted fields
                    Bakusui

Winter-solitary...
I find solace in this old
Chinese-painted pine

Basho

THE MOURNING FATHER

Deep under ashes...
Burning charcoal chilled now by
His hissing tears

Basho

In the rainy dawn
See where I crept out of bed...
Hole in the bedclothes

Joso

A mountain hamlet...
Under the great white snowdrift
A gurgling brook

Shiki

At freezing midnight
Hear that rat go rummaging ...
Dirty kitchen dishes
                    Buson

Even my lamp-light ...
Hibernating in a frozen
Winter-white halo
                    Yaha

Last night a snowfall ...
Today clear cobalt heaven and
White-mantled pines
                    Rokwa

A bitter night ... but
Long practice with cold hunger
Permitted me to sleep
                    Izen

Soft snowflakes settle
Down on these unstirring ducks...
A world of silence

Shiki

Wet snow is sweeping
Over the red-berry bush...
Two sparrows chirping

Shiki

Over and over
From my bed I ask my nurse:
Now, how deep the snow?

Shiki

At this dreary inn
A hound keeps wailing...like me
Lonely in the rain?

Basho

The very planets
Gleaming through its silhouette...
Frozen willow-tree

Chora

Every single star
Is quivering now with light...
O how bitter cold

Taigi

Bright soul of Winter...
Moonlight punctuated by
Pattering hailstones

Gyodai

Bitter Winter wind...
Won't it blow right off the sky
That day-old crescent?

Kakei

Now at dawn the tide
Floats incoming layers on
Our night-frozen cove
                    Shiki

Polishing the Buddha...
And why not my pipe as well
For the holiday?
                    Issa

On a rainy day
The dripping scarecrows seem like
Ordinary men
                    Seibi

Remembering
Their painted faces, she unwrapped
Her old pair of dolls
                    Buson

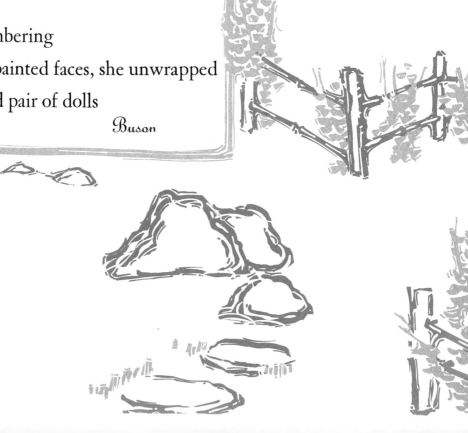

It is warm today...
But I think I feel the chill
Of that Winter sun

Onitsura

Children, come on out:
Clattering along the lane
See...it's hailing pearls

Basho

Icy Winter night...
I unfreeze the writing-brush
With my two good teeth

Buson

Out over the lake
Long cold hollow emptiness...
A solitary crow

Shiki

Those two tired dolls
In the corner there...ah yes,
They are man and wife

Issa

Silly hailstones...
Fleeing into my fireplace
Fast as they can run

Issa

In icy moonlight
Pin-point-pattering pebbles
Crunching underfoot

Buson

Cold Winter rain-lines
Are lifted horizontal
By the howling gale

Kyorai

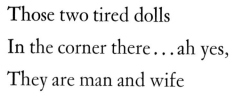

With his hat blown off
The solemn scarecrow stands here
Quite discomfited

Buson

Icy-winter night...
Perhaps the water-birds, like me,
Are lakeside huddlers

Rotsu

Darkening snow-clouds...
Over this waiting lake and land
Black birds whimpering

Otokuni

Blue-shadow-bolted...
The castle gate of Edo
In frozen moonlight

Kikaku

My neighbors hate me...
Hear them bang and rattle pans
In the icy night

     Buson

That snotty urchin
Left unpicked by either team...
Ah the bitter cold!

     Shiki

Before the Buddha
Even good sparrows bow...parents
And children both

     Issa

A harsh-rasping saw...
Music of cold poverty
In Winter midnight

     Buson

Year-end revelling...
Still in pilgrim's cape must I
Roam my endless road

Basho

Since dear Basho died
What poem-maker dares to write
"Year-end revelling"?

Buson

DEATH-SONG:

I was allotted
Two Autumns more than average
The harvest moon

Saikaku

DEATH-SONG:

On the last long road
When I fall and fail to rise...
I'll bed with flowers

Sora

Lonely umbrella
Passing the house at twilight...
First snow falling soft

Yaha

Carven gods long gone...
Dead leaves alone foregather
On the temple porch

Basho

Five or six of us
Remain, huddled together...
Bent old willow-trees

Kyorai

Plume of pampas grass
Trembling in every wind...
Hush, my lonely heart

Issa

Tea-water, tired
Waiting while we watched the snow
Froze itself a hat
                    Sokan

Cold first Winter rain...
Poor monkey, you too could use
A little woven cape
                    Basho

Winter rain deepens
Lichened letters on the grave...
And my old sadness
                    Roka

Cold Winter shower...
See all the people running
Across Seta Bridge!
                    Joso

Old weary willows...
How very long the road will be
When you fade away
                    Buson

No oil to read by...
I am off to bed but ah!...
My moonlit pillow
                    Basho

Descending seaward
Far-off mountain waterfall...
Winter nights are still
                    Kyokusui

All heaven and earth
Flowered white obliterate...
Snow...unceasing snow
                    Hashin

Considerate dogs...
Stepping off into the snow
As I walk the path

Issa

But when I halted
On the windy street at twilight...
Snow struck against me

Kito

Call him back! Ah no,
He's blown from sight already...
Fish-peddler in the snow

Anon.

Crossing it alone
In cold moonlight, the brittle bridge
Echoes my footsteps

Taigi

Such a little child
To send to be a priestling . . .
Icy poverty

              Shiki

Windy Winter rain . . .
My silly big umbrella
Tries walking backward

              Shisei-jo

Buddha on the hill . . .
From your holy nose indeed
Hangs an icicle

              Issa

This snowy morning
That black crow I hate so much . . .
But he's beautiful!

              Basho

Look at the candle!
What a hungry wind it is...
Hunting in the snow!

Seira

If there were fragrance
These heavy snowflakes settling...
Lilies on the rocks

Basho

Ah! I intended
Never never to grow old...
Listen: New Year's bell!

Jokun

Snow-swallowed valley:
Only the winding river...
Black fluent brushstroke

Boncho

Roaring Winter storm
Rushing to its utter end...
Ever-sounding sea

Gonsui

Eleven brave knights
Canter through the whirling snow
Not one bends his neck

Shiki

Going snow-viewing
One by one the walkers vanish...
Whitely falling veils

Katsuri

"Yes, come in!" I cried...
But at the windy snow-hung gate
Knocking still went on

Kyorai

See: surviving sons
Visit the ancestral grave...
Bearded, with bent canes

Basho

THE ORPHAN SPEAKS:

The year-end party...
I am even envious
Of scolded children

Issa

I gave the greetings
Of the bright New Year...as though
I held a plum-branch

Shiki

On jolly New Year's day
My last year's bills drop in
To pay their compliments

Anon.

DEATH-SONG:

Leaf alone, fluttering
Alas, leaf alone, fluttering...
Floating down the wind
Anon.

Snow whispering down
All day long, earth has vanished
Leaving only sky
Joso

Dusk, adrift at sea...
Why look back at those lesser
Hills hiding Fuji?
Kikaku

So cold are the waves
The rocking gull can scarcely
Fold itself to sleep
Basho

Twice perhaps three times
The chimes of the river changed...
Oh what a cold night!

Rokwa

That Winter when my
Faithless lover left me...
How cold the snow seemed

Jakushi

Ah the falling snow...
Imagine dancing butterflies flitting
Through the flakes!

Oemaru

The still snow we
Watched...will it cover our hill
Again this Winter?

Basho

Oh the first snowfall!
Who could stay indoors on such
A glorious day!

Kikaku

In stony moonlight
Hills and fields on every side
White and bald as eggs...

Ransetsu

Waking before dawn, see
How the constellations are all
Turned around!

Ransetsu

Even I who have
No lover...I love this time
Of new kimonos

Onitsura

How can a creature
Be so hated as a Winter fly
Yet live so long!

Kikaku

Hello! light the fire!
I'll bring inside a lovely
Bright ball of snow!

Basho

DEATH-SONG:

Three loveliest things:
Moonlight, cherry-bloom, now I go
Seeking silent snow

Rippo

DEATH-SONG:

Fever-felled half-way,
My dreams arose to march again...
Into a hollow land

Basho

DEATH-SONG:

I have known lovers...
Cherry-bloom...the nightingale...
I will sleep content

Anon.